IMAGES
of America

SEASIDE PARK

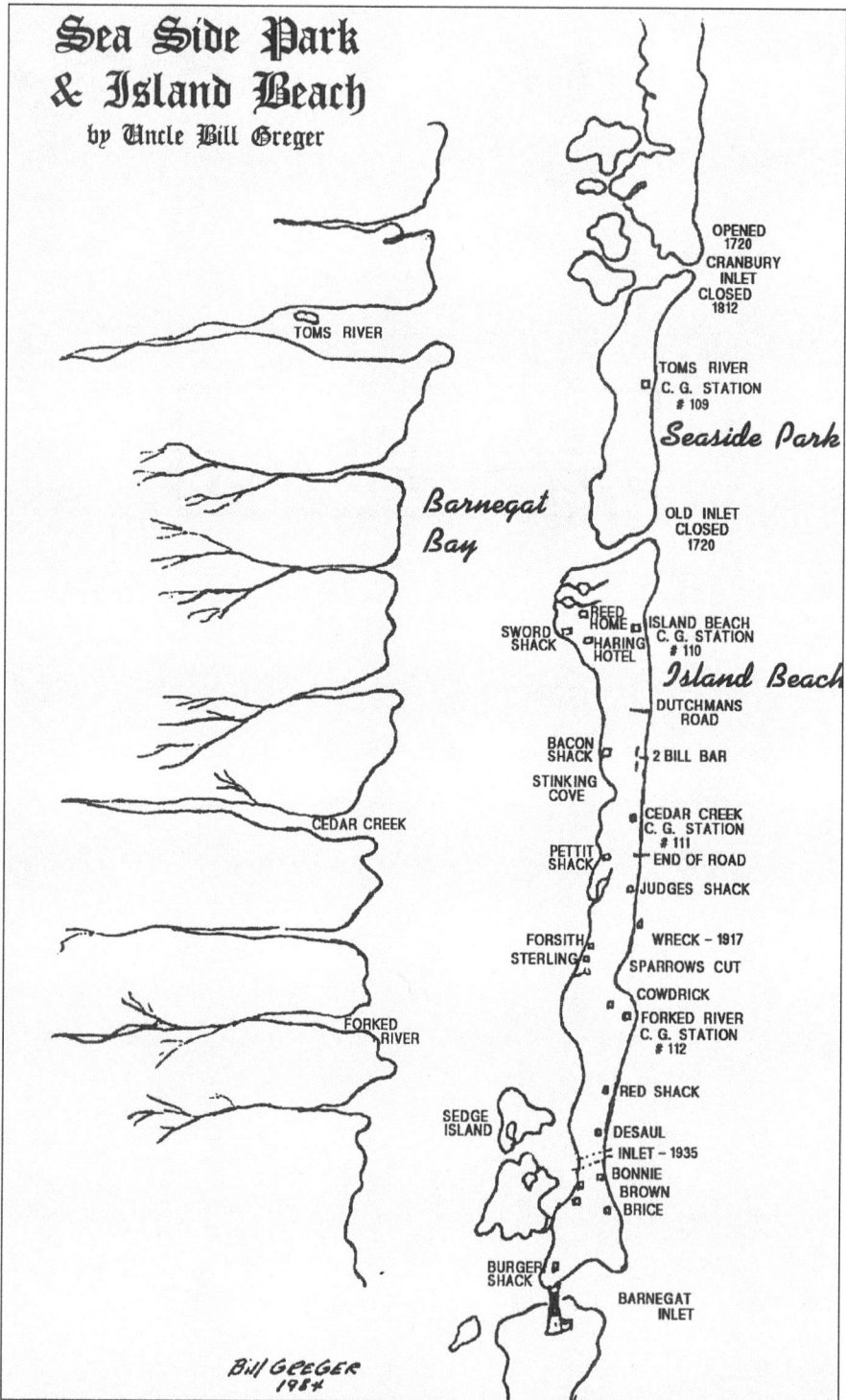

Sea Side Park & Island Beach
by Uncle Bill Greger

TOMS RIVER

Barnegat Bay

CEDAR CREEK

FORKED RIVER

SEDGE ISLAND

BURGER SHACK

Bill GREGER 1984

OPENED 1720 CRANBURY INLET CLOSED 1812

TOMS RIVER C. G. STATION # 109

Seaside Park

OLD INLET CLOSED 1720

REED HOME
SWORD SHACK
HARING HOTEL
ISLAND BEACH C. G. STATION # 110

Island Beach

DUTCHMANS ROAD

BACON SHACK
2 BILL BAR

STINKING COVE

CEDAR CREEK C. G. STATION # 111

PETTIT SHACK
END OF ROAD

JUDGES SHACK

FORSITH
STERLING
WRECK – 1917
SPARROWS CUT

COWDRICK
FORKED RIVER C. G. STATION # 112

RED SHACK

DESAUL
INLET – 1935
BONNIE
BROWN
BRICE

BARNEGAT INLET

The Coast Guard stations, old squatters' shacks, and inlets which once cut through the island are indicated on this map of Seaside Park and Island Beach made by the late "Uncle Bill" Greger. (Courtesy Barbara Greger.)

IMAGES
of America

SEASIDE PARK

Andrew J. Anderson

ARCADIA
PUBLISHING

Published by Arcadia Publishing
Charleston, South Carolina

Library of Congress Catalog Card Number: 2008922476

For all general information contact Arcadia Publishing at:
Telephone 843-853-2070
Fax 843-853-0044
E-mail sales@arcadiapublishing.com
For customer service and orders:
Toll-Free 1-888-313-2665

Visit us on the Internet at www.arcadiapublishing.com

The General Store, opened in 1881 by Franklin Harris, was the first market, post office, and town hall. It was located at Third and Central Avenues.

CONTENTS

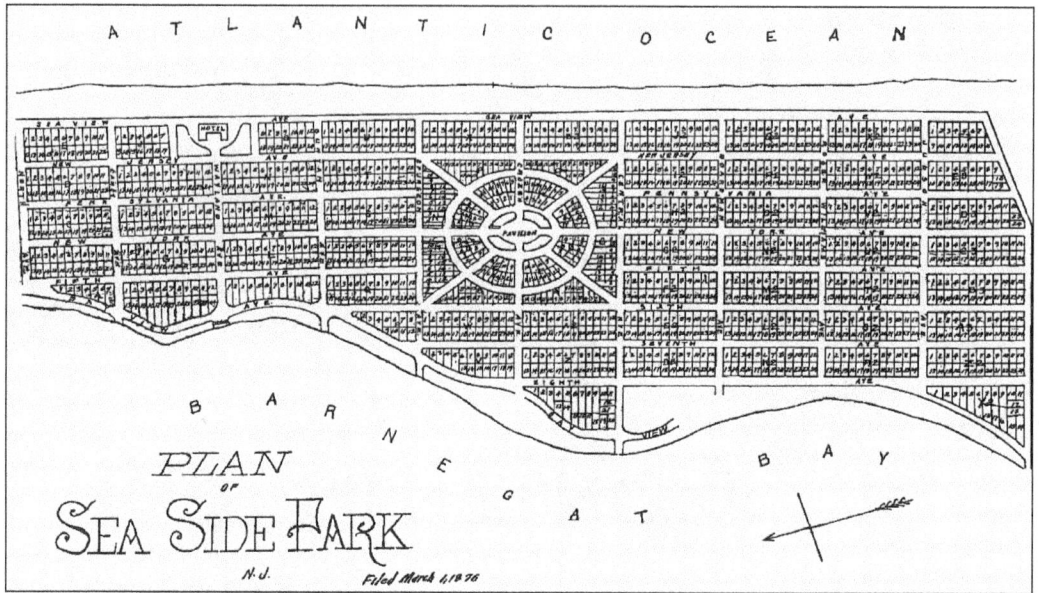

On the "Old Map" of the Baptist Sea Side Park Association, filed with the Ocean County Clerk's Office on March 1, 1876, the avenues ran north and south.

ACKNOWLEDGMENTS

The list of people who have contributed to making this book a reality is too numerous to itemize here. There are some special individuals who deserve special recognition. First and foremost, I thank my mother, D. Gail Anderson, for access to her extensive collection of photographs from Seaside Park's past. This is a collection which began in 1956 when, as a senior at Toms River High School, she wrote a term paper on the town and included a few old photographs. I have attempted to give credit to those who originally supplied the pictures to my family.

Additional information was provided by my grandmother, Edith Erwin, and father, Councilman Jesse Anderson. To them, I offer my gratitude and love.

I especially thank the Greger and Mueller families for making available the artwork of the late F. William "Uncle Bill" Greger. His line art drawings are synonymous with the history of Sea Side Park.

Ferd Klebold and the Ocean County Historical Society were both extremely supportive of this project. I also thank the dozens of locals who opened their photograph collections to me.

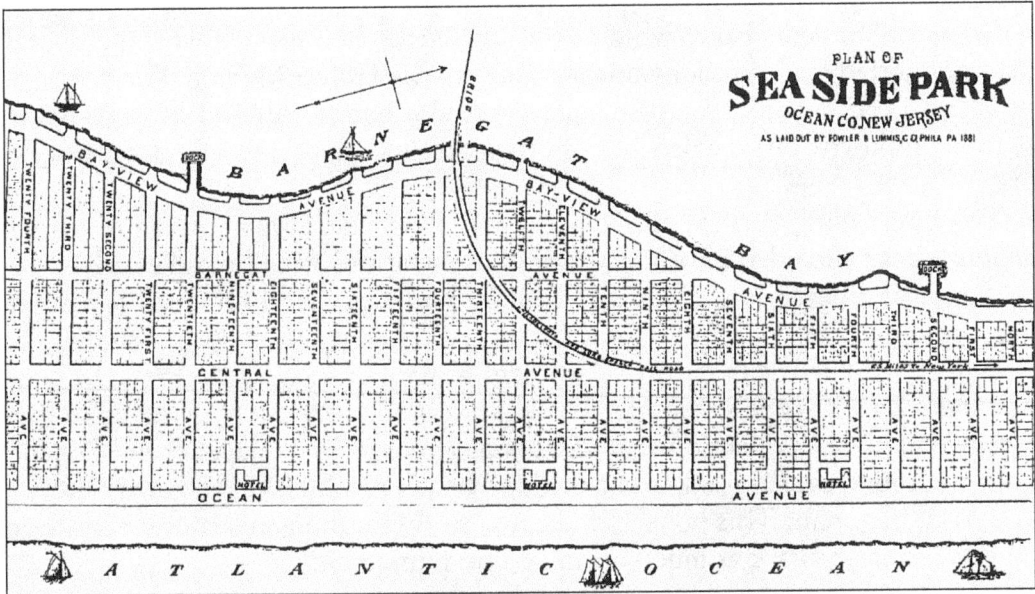

This is the "New Map" drawn up by the Thomas Kennedy family in 1881. The southern half of Seaside Park still follows this map.

INTRODUCTION

The borough of Seaside Park, originally spelled Sea Side Park, was incorporated in 1898. Located on the Barnegat Barrier Island in Ocean County, New Jersey, the small town has grown from a seasonal summer resort to a year-round community.

Grand hotels representative of the late gilded age were once the main attraction for vacationers from Philadelphia and New York. John Weaver, the first commodore of the Seaside Park Yacht Club, founded in 1899, later served as mayor of the City of Brotherly Love. The Pennsylvania Railroad carried passengers and freight into Seaside Park from 1881 until 1946. The railroad tracks and the colossal hotels are no more, replaced by the automobile and affordable motels.

The non-denominational Seaside Park Union Church, originally known as the "Chapel by the Sea," was built in 1899. A Catholic church, St. Catharine of Siena, soon followed. Both churches still have an active following.

School classes for this small town were first held in a room above the general store before the construction of a schoolhouse in 1902. A volunteer fire company and first aid squad were also established early on.

In South Seaside Park, which is a section of Berkeley Township, pound fisheries netted fresh fish for transportation to the Fulton Market. The borough of Island Beach, which is now a state park, also had hotels and an interesting seaweed industry. Little exists but photographs and memories of this long gone era.

The Life Saving Service played a key role in the development of the barrier island. I have included photographs of all the stations from Seaside Park south to Barnegat Inlet. Most of these buildings still exist, and are used for other purposes now.

I am the fourth generation of my family to live in Seaside Park. I chose pictures which were representative of what my ancestors saw growing up in this family resort. The collection includes aerial photographs, images of old Seaside Park with its graveled road, and artwork by the late Bill Greger, town butcher and local historian. This book is dedicated to the future generations, that they may love Seaside Park as much as those who founded it.

Andrew J. Anderson
Sea Side Park, New Jersey
Summer 1998

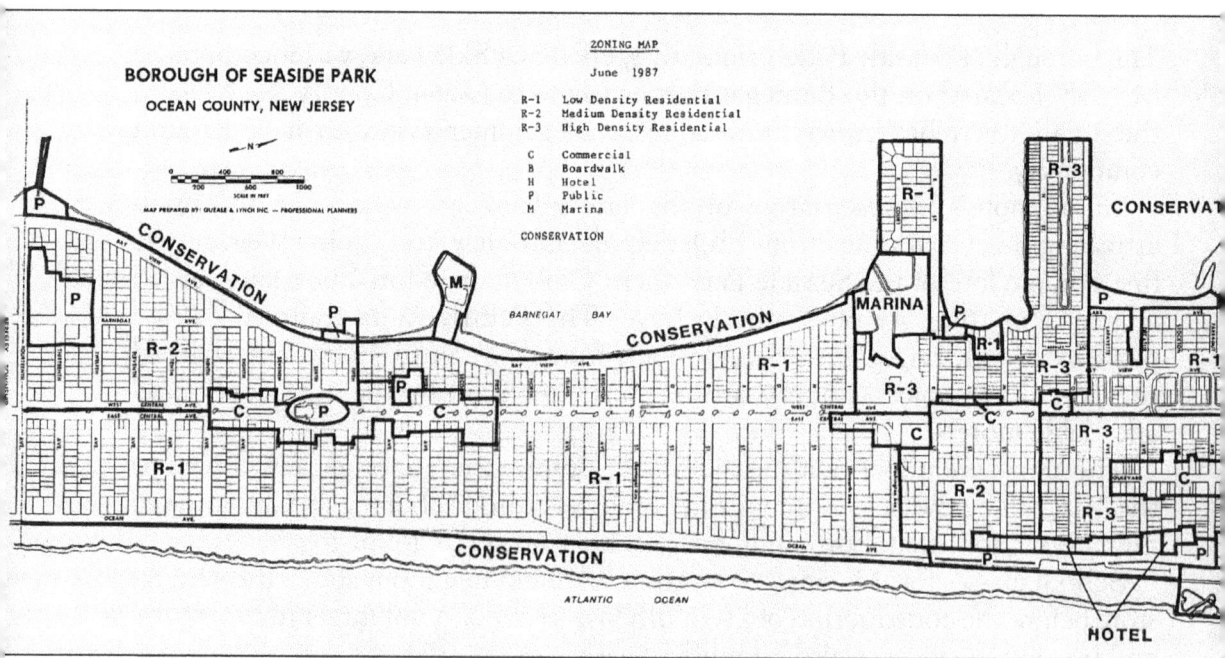

Shown here is the borough of Seaside Park as it is today.

One

THE LIFE SAVING SERVICE

Dr. William A. Newell, a congressman from Manahawkin, New Jersey, introduced an amendment to an existing lighthouse bill on August 9, 1854, and established the Life Saving Service. At first the stations were privately operated, but the federal government took them over in 1881. They were established approximately every 3 to 5 miles along the New Jersey coast. Toms River Station No. 13 was originally located at Decatur Avenue and the Boulevard in Seaside Park. Getting ready for a boat drill at the Toms River Life Saving Station are, from left to right, Peter Newman, Phineas Potter, Tom Wilbur, Fred Bailey, and Sam Dunham. (Courtesy June Roy.)

The original Toms River Life Saving Service Station No. 13, as photographed about 1898 by Norman McClure of Toms River, was a small cottage. The station was manned from September 15 through April 15, when the Atlantic Ocean was at its fiercest. From left to right are Captain Elwood Rogers, Thomas Wilbur, Dillon Wilbur, Charles Bozier, Peter Newman, James Applegate, Joe Smires, and George Everingham. (Courtesy June Roy.)

Some of the old-timers at the Toms River Life Saving Station included, from left to right, Jim Applegate, Sam Dunham, Captain Henry Ware, Tom Wilbur, Fred Bailey, and Frank Brockway. (Courtesy June Roy.)

A larger station was built on the oceanfront at Decatur Avenue between 1898 and 1900. The inside of the station consisted of a kitchen and one large room on the main floor with a big, long table where the crew ate their meals. There were seven men in the crew, and each man took his turn cooking. The second floor of the building was one spacious room where each man had a bed and a foot locker. From the tower the watch would look for ships through binoculars. (Courtesy Dorothy Thomas.)

Toms River Life Saving Service Station crewmen included, from left to right, Tom Wilbur, Sam Dunham, Lester Brower, Pete Newman, Fred Bailey, and Captain Wilbur. The boats were kept along the side of the building. The crew would drill with the breeches buoy and the men would practice upsetting the boats and righting them again. (Courtesy Anna Brower.)

William Marren is seen here with his dogs on Eleventh Avenue. The small building in the background was a half-way stop for station foot patrols. These buildings were located between the stations and were a meeting place for the nighttime patrols, who would exchange chits as proof they had completed their walk to the building. (Courtesy Betty Perinchief.)

In 1915, the Life Saving Service and the United States Treasury Department's Cutter Service were merged to form the Coast Guard. Toms River Life Saving Station No. 13 was renamed Coast Guard Station No. 109. The station was closed in July 1964, and sold to the borough two years later. In 1996, the municipal offices were moved into the historic building. (Courtesy June Roy.)

12

Island Beach Life Saving Station No. 14, c. 1897, was located 4 miles south of the Toms River Station. The building was sold to the Sword family when the newer station was built in 1898. From left to right are Captain Joe F. Reed, Bert Reed, Mr. Campbell, C. Tilton, J. Potter, Ben Newman, unidentified, Ed Miller, R. Penn, and E. Penn. (Courtesy Bill Greger.)

The Island Beach Station was renamed No. 110 after the formation of the Coast Guard. Here, the crew is returning from a boat drill. The life preservers worn by the men were made of cloth filled with cork. (Courtesy Harold Wilkins.)

The new Island Beach Coast Guard Station No. 110 was of a traditional design. Captain Lewis Mitchell was the last captain to serve the station, from the 1920s until the station went out of service in 1948. It is now located in Island Beach State Park, and is a stop on the New Jersey Coastal Heritage Trail.

The crew of Island Beach Station No. 110, c. 1919, were, from left to right, Cale Worth, George Worth, Harold Wilkins, Edgar Sexton, Mr. Jones, and Russell Penn. Here, they have just returned from one of their numerous boat and rescue drills. (Courtesy Harold Wilkins.)

The men in the Life Saving Service excelled at their duties. They were vigorously put through various tests, including the breeches buoy test and that of launching, capsizing, and righting a lifeboat in a heavy surf, before a large crowd of spectators. Pictured here is Superintendent John S. Cole conducting an annual inspection drill at Island Beach, c. 1919. Russell Penn is the man in center, and Harold Wilkins is to the right holding the time watch. (Courtesy Harold Wilkins.)

Cedar Creek Life Saving Station No. 15 was built 5 miles south of the Island Beach Station in 1872. Built by Cottrell, Gallup, and Company of Mystic, Connecticut, it was later altered in 1884 and 1907–08, when the windows were added on the upper story. It became U.S. Coast Guard Station No. 111 in 1915. The station closed in 1937 and was later demolished by the State of New Jersey.

Forked River Life Saving Station No. 16, later Coast Guard Station No. 112, was built in 1854 about 1.5 miles north of Barnegat Inlet. The steel lookout tower was built east of the station in 1929, with the present building (shown here) built in 1932. It is now an Interpretive Center for the state park. (Courtesy June Roy.)

The sole survivors of a shipwreck off Barnegat Inlet are seen here warming themselves in the kitchen of Forked River Coast Guard Station No. 112. The coast of New Jersey was often called the graveyard of the Atlantic because of all the shipwrecks which occurred there.

The breeches buoy was a lifesaving device used to take persons off ships at sea. It hung from a pulley that ran from ship to ship or ship to shore. Another line was used to pull the buoy along the pulley line. The passenger sat in a cork ring with his legs in canvas breeches. Shown here, the life savers are rescuing the crew from the *Thermon* on Christmas Day 1909. The men were brought in first, followed by the smoke stack. Doors were put on both ends of the smoke stack and the rescued men lived in there on the beach. No lives were lost. (Courtesy Frances Baker.)

In March 1906, the *Cearance*, sailing from Brazil to New York with a cargo of nuts, rubber, and sugar cane, ran aground off Twelfth Avenue. Tugs freed the ship within a week and towed it to New York. Two "Parksonians," including soon-to-be mayor A. Carl Haag Sr., were on board the *Cearance* as it journeyed to New York. (Courtesy Anna Brower.)

The *Sarah Blaisdell* was ransacked after its beaching in the summer of 1928. (Courtesy Betty Perinchief.)

On April 8, 1943, the *Annie & Rubin*, sailing from New York and heading for South America without being cleared by customs, was beached south of the Island Beach Coast Guard Station by her captain after she sprang a leak that could not be taken care of by her pumps. She carried a mixed cargo consisting of women's silk stockings, night gowns, panties, and pajamas; bolts of drapery and upholstering material, rayon, and taffeta; and toilet accessories, paints, lacquers, Coca-Cola syrup, and liquor.

Two

THE PENNSYLVANIA RAILROAD

On July 4, 1881, the Pennsylvania Railroad made its historic first run from Philadelphia through Sea Side Park, crossing the newly completed train bridge which linked the town with the mainland. The first railroad station was in the Hiawatha Hotel. In 1882, the station shown here was built between Fifth and Sixth Avenues. With the advent of the railroad, it became possible to ship fresh fish to the markets in Philadelphia. Market owners were soon traveling to the city to purchase various produce items from wholesalers. (Courtesy Richard Steele.)

The Sea Side Park Railroad Station was located near the Seaside Park Hotel, which was later renamed the Manhasset Hotel. It cost 50¢ to have a trunk carried from the railroad station to the hotel or from the hotel to the station. (Courtesy Gary Madden.)

The Hewitt & Son express wagon often waited at the train station for deliveries. The horses were also used by the fire company until the borough purchased their own team. (From the postcard collection of Robert Irons, courtesy Gary Madden.)

During the late 1800s and early 1900s, residents and visitors walked along gravel roads to reach the train station. Seen in the background on the left is the freight siding. Homes were widespread with side streets often no more than wide sandy pathways indicating where graveled streets would later be constructed. An early street light can be seen on the pole to the right. (Courtesy Dorothy Thomas.)

The Sea Side Park Railroad Station was also known by the code "PK," as seen here on the overhang. The vender in front of the station sold newspapers, magazines, comic books, and penny candy to the passengers and townsfolk alike. (Courtesy Stella Brown.)

The railroad helped support the fishing industry which grew along the New Jersey shore. This 750-pound horse mackerel was caught at Seaside Park. The view is looking north from the railroad station. (Courtesy Gary Madden.)

The jitney on the right was owned by E.C. Flitcroft, owner of the Modern Garage. He ran a taxi service between 1911 and 1924, carrying people from the train station and on sight-seeing tours. His jitneys were used for first aid duty as well, taking sick and injured people to the doctor. (Courtesy Gary Madden.)

As homes sprang up in the northern section of town, a train stop was created at Stockton Avenue to accommodate residents arriving from New York, north Jersey, and the Philadelphia–Camden areas. (Courtesy Gary Madden.)

An E6-type Pennsylvania Railroad locomotive is seen here coming off the trestle at Fourteenth Avenue, Seaside Park, in July 1939. Rail cars had a potbellied stove in one corner for heat. After checking tickets, the conductor would keep the fire going in the stove. (Courtesy Gary Madden.)

BARNEGHT PIER N.J
1910

Stella Hewitt Brown was on her way home from high school when this terrible accident occurred. The brakeman threw the wrong switch and the result was a head-on collision between a freight and passenger train. The engineer and fireman on the passenger train were both killed. (Courtesy Stella Brown.)

The Pennsylvania Railroad maintained a freight yard near Twelfth and Central Avenues. Called the "wye," this was a Y-shaped piece of property where a short spur branched south and went to the fish pounds in South Seaside Park. The maintenance car shown here was destroyed by fire just north of the wye, between Tenth and Eleventh Avenues.

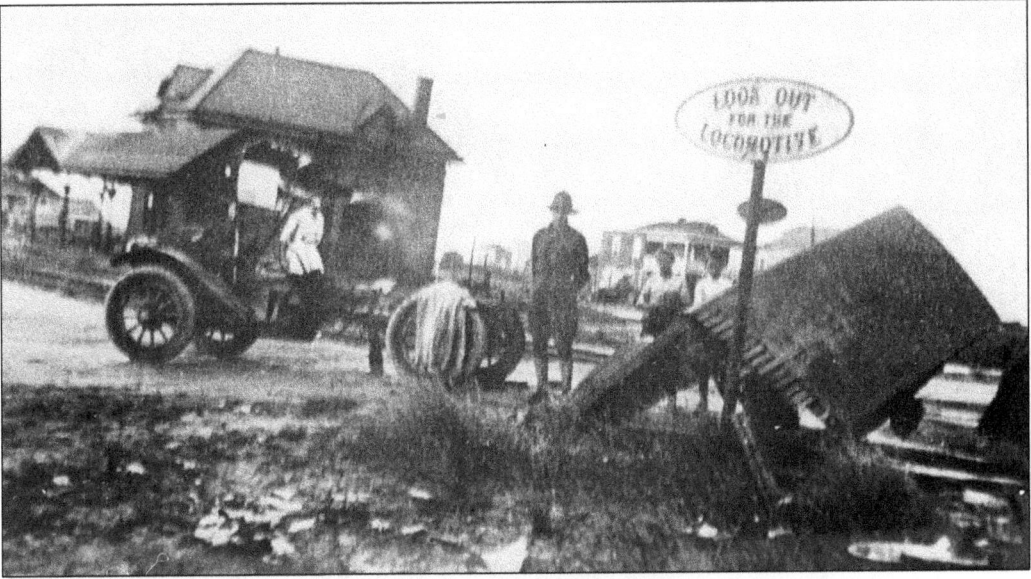

Automobile and pedestrian accidents were not all that commonplace, but they did occur. This accident was at J Street, c. 1918. In the background is the Berkeley Station, built in the late 1800s to service the Berkeley Arms Hotel. In August 1933, Mrs. Florence Wilkins was instantaneously killed by a train while crossing at Third Avenue. (Courtesy Bill Greger.)

Ice was a constant problem during the winter. As seen here, there was a tremendous ice build-up on the trestle as Barnegat Bay froze. (Courtesy Stella Brown.)

In the winter of 1913, a frigid cold spell and unprecedented ice flow destroyed 600 feet of the Pennsylvania Railroad Bridge and mangled the tracks. The Island Heights and Sea Side Park Bridge, under construction 2 miles north of the trestle, was also severely damaged. (Courtesy Stella Brown.)

Workmen repaired the Pennsylvania Railroad Bridge in 1913. The newly built automobile bridge also had to be repaired. (Courtesy Stella Brown.)

Barnegat Pier, located at the draw on the Pennsylvania Railroad Bridge, was a popular place for sailboats to dock. (Courtesy Frances Hodulich Baker.)

On December 1, 1946, an early-morning fire incinerated 300 feet of the Pennsylvania Railroad Bridge, destroying the pilings and timbers and ending train transportation from Camden and Philadelphia to Seaside Park. After a public hearing, the Pennsylvania Railroad abandoned their tracks and trestle. The remains of the bridge were turned into a fishing and crabbing dock in the 1950s.

The abandoned railroad tracks were removed from Seaside Park beginning August 20, 1949, to make more room for Central Avenue and parking spaces. This railroad car for the American Legion was also transported down the streets of Seaside Park in 1949. (Courtesy June Roy.)

This is the Seaside Park Railroad Station as it appeared on January 18, 1954. The building was purchased by Albert A. Lukaisch for $50 in 1952 and moved to Eleventh and Central Avenues. It is now used as apartments. The Seaside Park Town Hall was built at the former site of the railroad station at Sixth and Central Avenues and was dedicated in 1953. (Courtesy Guy Mueller.)

Three

THE ISLAND HEIGHTS AND SEA SIDE PARK BRIDGE

The first automobile bridge connecting Seaside Park with Toms River was the Bay Bridge. Built by the Island Heights and Sea Side Park Bridge Company, under the leadership of such influential men as Francis P. Larkin, Christian T. Hiering, William Cummings, and Judge Edwin H. Berry, this span was originally a toll bridge. The State of New Jersey purchased the bridge on March 1, 1922, and abolished the tolls. It was extensively rebuilt and widened in 1926, reopening with an extravagant 7-mile-long parade on May 28, 1927.

While the Bay Bridge was under construction, the *Ariella* and the *Dorianna* carried passengers to Toms River and back. The Island Heights and Sea Side Park Bridge, as the Bay Bridge was officially known, was designed by engineer Arthur C. King and built by the F.R. Long and W.G. Broadhurst Co. of Hackensack, New Jersey.

The building of the Bay Bridge was not to be accomplished without dramatic incident. The bridge was scheduled to open on Friday, March 13, 1914. The bridge committee gave formal acceptance and settlement was to be made the following Saturday. During this short interval, huge ice blocks ripped 1,100 feet out of the bridge, which had no ice breakers. It would be another year before automobiles would cross Barnegat Bay. .

The final cost of the 21-foot-wide bridge was $153,447.90. The bridge was road level at each end and about 10 feet at the draw. The draw was 50 feet long and the bascule, 125 tons of concrete and steel, was so balanced it could easily be raised or lowered by one man. The tollhouse with its machinery cost $1,935; legal and other fees cost $21,741; taxes were $912; and the government license was $1,239. Arthur C. King, the engineer, received $5,589.

Tolls for the Bay Bridge in 1915 were as follows: pleasure cars and drivers, 25¢, with each additional passenger, 5¢; trucks, light or loaded, under 3 tons, 50¢; trucks over 3 tons, $1; sightseeing cars, 50¢; motorcycles, 15¢; horse and driver, 15¢; pedestrian, 10¢; each horse, cattle, hog, or sheep, led or in droves, 10¢; and a pedestrian with a wheelbarrow, 15¢.

On October 26, 1948, construction began on the Thomas Mathis Bridge. The concrete span, built at a cost of $7 million, was 28 feet wide with two lanes and a draw. The bridge, located just south of the original bridge, was dedicated on March 24, 1950, in honor of the centennial of Ocean County. The wooden Bay Bridge was soon demolished.

Ted Jerstad and Alex Svurndland, carpenters from Norway, enjoy the view of Barnegat Bay. A second bridge, named after Seaside Heights Mayor J. Stanley Tunney, was built at the site of the first Bay Bridge in 1970. The Thomas Mathis and the J. Stanley Tunney Bridges are now the major arteries to and from Seaside Park.

Four

HOTELS

During the 1870s, Sea Side Park was becoming a well-liked summer resort. To accommodate the tourists, some of the grandest hotels to be found on the eastern seaboard were built on the narrow barrier island. One of the first and largest hotels was the Seaside Park Hotel. Built in 1875, it was remodeled and renamed the Manhasset by the turn of the century to "savor the old Indian connections in this neighborhood." The Manhasset was built 6 feet off the ground. Bricks for the structure were brought from the mainland in boats. Charlie Bozeth, known to the locals as old Captain Boshier, was one of the men who carted the bricks. His boat would carry some 1,000 bricks into a channel located at Fifth Avenue. After he brought a load over in the morning, horses and wagons would carry the bricks to the oceanfront where the hotel was being constructed. This would usually take the rest of the day. (Courtesy Robert Haag.)

The Manhasset covered the entire oceanfront block between Fourth and Fifth Avenues and could accommodate 300 people. It contained 133 guest rooms, 29 private baths, 33 rooms with running water only, 3 converted rooms with running water plus toilets, a dining room with large windows overlooking the Atlantic, and a ballroom with an orchestra for dancing on the main floor. (Courtesy Anna Brower.)

The dining room of the Manhasset Hotel, as sketched in a 1904 advertising brochure, reminded one of "dining at sea," with first-class service, experienced waiters, and music during luncheon and dinner hours. Particular attention was given to the cuisine, with each department in the charge of a specialist. The dining and ballrooms were both illuminated by electric lights.

The Manhasset Hotel was destroyed by fire on Easter Sunday, 1931. The Manhasset blaze, at the time, was the borough's largest conflagration. The fire raged from 1 a.m. to 4:30 a.m. and caused $350,000 damage. Destroyed were the hotel and four summer cottages; the fire also damaged the Hotel Gladwyn and a dozen more cottages.

Approximately 25 fire companies from Ocean County and southern Monmouth County responded with 35 units to the nighttime blaze, which was visible from as far north as Long Branch. Homeowners attacked the fire with brooms and buckets of water; 80 people were injured. The Citizens' Association of Seaside Park gave a dinner of appreciation to the firemen on April 24, 1931, at the Bay View Inn.

The Berkeley Arms Hotel was built in 1883 by George M. Dorrance. It was opened with a splurge of newspaper fanfare, partly by the fact that it was first managed by George C. Boldt, then of the Stratford Hotel, but afterward of the Bellevue in Philadelphia, and Waldorf-Astoria in New York. The first year it was open was known as the "mosquito year," as clouds of those pests were thicker that year than for a long time before or after.

The Berkeley Arms, being located in the low ground on the oceanfront between I and J Streets, fell victim to the mosquitoes that drove away the high-priced guests that George C. Boldt had gathered. That was the start of 20 years of failure. On July 12, 1904, the hotel was destroyed by fire. Furniture rescued from the hotel was later sold at auction.

All that remained of the Berkeley Arms by 1917 was the Spring House. The pure water from the well was believed to have medicinal value. Today, the site of the Spring House is now the location of the Tri-Boro First Aid Squad Building. (Courtesy Harnett B. Donaldson.)

The Gladwyn Hotel was built in the early 1900s on the south side of Sixth Avenue. It was convenient to the train depot, beaches, the Seaside Park Yacht Club, and pier. The hotel advertised that all rooms had an ocean or bay view. The piazzas were high and wide, affording comfortable lounging places during the heat of the day or for a social hour in the air during the evening. On the American or European plan, the Gladwyn provided "plain food carefully prepared to keep you well and help you recover your health if you are sick." Rates were $4 per day and $22.50 per week. (Courtesy Ferd & Nancy Klebold.)

The Hiawatha Hotel had its beginnings with the Centennial of the United States in 1876. It was first known as the Maryland House, one of the buildings erected by the 13 original states for the celebration that was taking place in South Philadelphia. The hotel was floated down from the old Centennial Grounds and moved to Sea Side Park about 1878. The building arrived in 2 sections on barges. It was unloaded at the bay shore and skidded to between First and Second Avenues on East Central Avenue. (Courtesy Miriam Anteau.)

The Hiawatha served as the first train station in 1881 and one of the first post offices in town. By the turn of the century, the hotel was thoroughly renovated, refurbished, and wired for electric lights. (Courtesy Anna Brower.)

In 1947, the hotel was purchased by Lawrence Cella, who renamed it the Ocean Tide. The uneven foundation was re-leveled and a restaurant and pub, the Ship's Bar, was attached to the north side of the building. (Courtesy Joe & Rosemarie Cella.)

Breakfast and dinner, cooked by Kerful Carter, a "superb" chef from Virginia, were included in the cost of the rooms at the Ocean Tide. Lawrence Cella owned and operated the Ocean Tide until his passing in 1963. With the changing economy, the large hotel could not operate solely on its seasonal business. The 88-year-old building was demolished in 1964. A decade later, the Windjammer Motor Lodge was built on the site. (Courtesy Joe and Rosemarie Cella.)

Built in the early 1900s, the Strand Hotel was a Seaside Park landmark through several generations. A hotel and restaurant, the Strand also offered guests dressing rooms for bathing, hot and cold showers, and private lockers at the rear of the building. By the late 1980s, the Strand was falling into financial difficulties and the building was in disrepair. Carl and Mary Ann Palmisano purchased the dilapidated building and had it razed. The Victorian-style home built on the corner of Ocean and North Avenues is appropriately named "On the Strand." (Courtesy Robert Magee.)

Kittatinny Hotel Seaside Park, N. J.

The Kittatinny, located on First Avenue and built about 1914, offered home comforts and would provide a room by the day for $1.50–$2, or for a weekly rate of $8, $10, or $12, in 1916. The hotel had three floors of rooms above a main floor consisting of a kitchen, dining room, and porch. It was built with used lumber brought from Philadelphia. The Kittatinny was sold to the Brick Township-based Greenbriar Corporation and demolished on Monday, July 22, 1974. (Courtesy Ferd and Nancy Klebold.)

Five

THE SEASIDE PARK YACHT CLUB

The Seaside Park Yacht Club was incorporated on August 29, 1899. Henry J. West, a bay front cottager, inaugurated a series of sneak box races on Barnegat Bay for large cash prizes. As a result of these races, there developed a strong tendency toward the formation of a regular yacht club. A meeting of cottage owners and yachtsmen in Sea Side Park was held and the Seaside Park Yacht Club was immediately formed. The clubhouse was built the following year at the foot of Second Avenue. (Courtesy Ferd and Nancy Klebold.)

The Honorable John Weaver was elected first commodore of the Seaside Park Yacht Club. He served as commodore from 1899 until 1906, and again from 1910 until 1912. John Weaver was mayor of Philadelphia from 1904 until 1908. The first board of directors was composed of the leading yachting enthusiasts such as Henry J. West, Harry B. Wyeth, John E. Creth, Dr. George H. Thacher, George S. Gandy, and Harvey T. Weber. (Courtesy SPYC.)

The clubhouse was formally opened at 11:30 a.m. on Saturday, July 21, 1900, when H.B. Wyeth, chairman of the building committee, in an appropriate address turned the house over to Commodore John Weaver, as the representative of the club. The clubhouse was designed by J. Elvin Jackson of Philadelphia and was built over Barnegat Bay some 250 feet from shore.

42

As seen here in 1902, the clubhouse has three floors. The first floor was a boat floor in which row boats and smaller sailboats were kept. The second floor had a large reception hall running the whole width of the house, a large room containing shuffle boards, billiard and pool tables, a ladies' reception room, gentlemen's smoking room, and toilet rooms. The third floor was a large assembly room with a stage and dressing room, and a committee room in the corner tower. (Courtesy John Haas.)

Racing has always been part of the tradition of the yacht club. On July 21, 1900, the Honorable William J. Sewell, a U.S. Senator from New Jersey, presented a sterling silver trophy cup to be sailed for annually on the second Saturday of August. (Courtesy Dorothy Thomas.)

This view of the Seaside Park Yacht Clubhouse, as seen from Barnegat Bay in 1906, shows the variety of boats members owned. The porch around the clubhouse is lined with hundreds of people eager to watch an upcoming race. (Courtesy Mike Mangum.)

Boating attire was quite formal in the early 1900s. Because it was sacrilegious to spoil their complexions, ladies would carry a parasol to protect them from the sun. (Courtesy Mike Mangum.)

Before the Race.   SEASIDE PARK, N. J.

Simply titled "Before the Race," this postcard demonstrates the excitement of all those involved in participating and viewing the weekend races during the warm summer months. (Courtesy Mike Mangum.)

The Regatta Committee, seen here about 1910, posed on the steps to the clubhouse. (Courtesy John Haas.)

The *Tamwock*, one of the original five class-A cat boats, was originally owned by Francis P. Larkin and sailed by Francis P. Larkin Jr. Designed by architect Francis S. Sweisguth, the *Tamwock* was built by John Kirk of Toms River. On May 7, 1940, the boat was destroyed in a boatyard fire in Island Heights. A model of the *Tamwock* is on display at the Philadelphia Maritime Museum. (Courtesy Jean Larkin.)

Francis P. Larkin Sr. displays trophies won by the *Tamwock* in 1926. Included are six first-place cups, two second-place cups, and two third-place cups. He also owned the *Dorothy*, one of the original cat boats to race on Barnegat Bay. The *Dorothy* won the Sewell Cup in 1913. (Courtesy Francis P. "Sonny" and Dorothy Larkin III.)

46

These trophies were all won by the *Dorothy* in 1911. (Courtesy James McFillin.)

The original five class-A cat boats were, from left to right, *Lotus*, *Bat*, *Mary Ann*, *Spy*, and *Tamwock*. In 1914, Seaside Park Yacht Club Commodore Herman Muller was instrumental in the formation of the Barnegat Bay Yacht Racing Association. Commodore Muller was elected secretary. Since 1914, six of the association commodores have been chosen from the Seaside Park Yacht Club. (Courtesy Jean Larkin.)

Owing to the immense popularity of the yacht club, a larger and more commodious house was needed and with very little difficulty funds were raised and a large addition made to the clubhouse. The roof lines of the original clubhouse can still be seen, with the addition on the south of the structure. (Courtesy Richard Steele.)

Cat boats, seen here moored at the yacht club dock in 1902, were very popular during the turn of the century. (Courtesy William Schoettle.)

By July 1918, the area between the Seaside Park Yacht Club and Bayview Avenue had been bulkheaded and filled in. A swimming pool was once located in front of the clubhouse. The diving board was installed in 1934. This photograph had the simple caption "Honk, honk!" written on it, as the young sailor is ready to go to the clubhouse. (Courtesy Jean Larkin.)

The summer of 1916, when this photograph was taken, was an exciting time in Seaside Park. The yacht club and the board of trade sponsored spectacular events for the Fourth of July, including water sports and sneak box races, culminating in a fireworks display and dancing at the Manhasset Hotel. (Courtesy Dorothy Thomas.)

The Seaside Park Yacht Club has always been the hub of social activity in Seaside Park. Tennis, an activity very popular with the younger members of the club, was played in these courts located in front of the clubhouse. This area is now parking for the members. The social features of the club were many. The entertainment provided by the Ladies Auxiliary included cabarets, dances, card parties, and musical entertainment staged every Friday and Saturday evening. (Courtesy Ferd and Nancy Klebold.)

Six

BUSINESSES

The Colonial Theater, on the southwest corner of Stockton Avenue and the Boulevard, opened on Saturday, July 1, 1916, with showings of Charlie Chaplin's *Work* and director James Kirkwood's *Rags*. The theater was advertised as "well ventilated and well screened, with six exits and of fire resisting construction." The building was 34 by 81 feet and seated 450 comfortably. Albert C. Lewis, who already owned the town's lumberyard, opened the theater with the promise of only "up to date pictures." To encourage moviegoers to attend showings, transportation was provided to the theater from the Seaside Park Post Office and Seaside Heights, for a 3¢ fare each way. Ed Newman drove the jitney bus. The photo-play operator was William Greene. (Courtesy Ellen Marzulli.)

The Hewitt and Son Express Office was located on the southwest corner of Central and Fifth Avenues. In the background is the Haag Block, including his ice cream parlor and real estate office. (Courtesy Stella Brown.)

Frank Hewitt's express wagon is seen here in front of the old Meadow House at 122 Ninth Avenue. The home of Hon. and Mrs. Russell Conover was demolished in the 1980s. Two duplexes were built on the lots in 1998. (Courtesy Stella Brown.)

The Hewitt and Son Express Office was later moved to Sixth and East Central Avenues, next to the Hewitt Realty Corporation, for use as an ice storage house. By 1930, there was a fleet of ice trucks belonging to Hewitt. (Courtesy Millard Erwin.)

Hewitt and Son hired many local men, including, from left to right, Edward Withers, Alfred Erwin, Edgar "Reds" Caskery, Frank Hewitt, Edgar Graham, Roy Lyman, and Millard Erwin. The men are seen here in front of the Hewitt Realty Corporation in 1930. (Courtesy Millard Erwin.)

The Haag Block, Fifth and Central Avenues, had a real estate office, ice cream parlor, and post office. A. Carl Haag was mayor from 1908 until 1912. He was one of the "Parksonians" who traveled to New York City on the SS *Cearance* after the ship ran aground off Seaside Park. (Courtesy Gary Madden.)

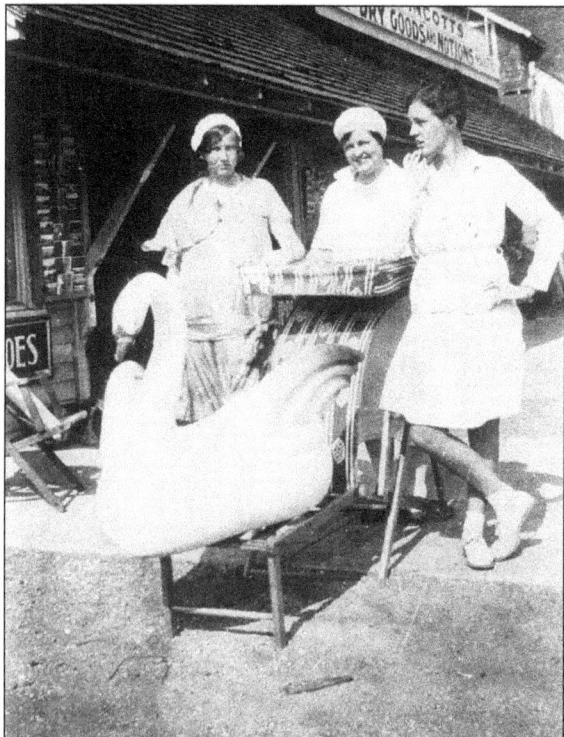

Opened in 1915, Lippincott's Store on the north side of Fifth Avenue sold toys, dry goods and notions, fishing and crabbing equipment, and the most complete postcard selection to be found in the area. Horace Lippincott Sr. was the railroad stationmaster, mayor from 1921 until 1923, and an early member of the volunteer fire company. His wife, Margaret, later served as postmistress from 1935 through 1952. Cowdrick's Garage was located to the right of the store. (Courtesy Horace Lippincott.)

Stores on Fifth Avenue included Lippincott's Store, Alfred Mathis's real estate office, and Carl Haag's block. The Abbott's Ice Cream sign was located near the Bay View Inn, a favorite restaurant and gathering place for both locals and tourists. (Courtesy Charles Martowlis.)

Anthony "Andy" Wickham greets customers as they enter his pharmacy at Third and Central Avenues. The drug store was located in the house built by Franklin Harris, who opened the first general store in Sea Side Park at that location in 1881. The building was demolished in 1927 when Central Avenue was widened. (Courtesy Ferd and Nancy Klebold.)

The Bazaar, located at Fifth and Central, sold toys, Japanese goods, sporting goods, Native-American blankets, needlework, clothing, souvenirs, and postcards. In the background is the Manhasset Hotel. The fence rail on the right is from the railroad station. This picture was taken c. 1909.

Aaron "Duffy" Wilbert and Ernest H. Boekholt purchased the Bazaar storefront in 1930 and opened the E & D Store, short for Ernest and Duffy. When Ernest Boekholt became the sole owner the following year, he changed the name to B & B, for Boekholt and Boekholt, after himself and son James. (Courtesy James Boekholt.)

Fifth and Bayview Avenues was the site of Penn's Cafe, operated by Mrs. Ed Penn during the early 1900s. Penn's was the predecessor of the Bay View Inn. Over the years the building was expanded to the large restaurant seen here. Many dinners and banquets were held at the Bay View, including the dinner of appreciation to all the firemen involved in fighting the Manhasset Hotel blaze on Easter Sunday 1931. (Courtesy Sterling Flitcroft.)

On January 10, 1970, fire destroyed the Bayview Lodge. The restaurant was rebuilt, but was destroyed again in a terrifying daytime blaze in July 1985. The historic landmark was not to be rebuilt a second time. (Courtesy Ed Laird.)

The old school bus is parked in front of E.C. Flitcroft's Garage and Auto Supply Station, North and Central Avenues. Elliot Flitcroft transported nine students to the Toms River High School for the sum of $828; each additional student cost $92. (Courtesy Sterling Flitcroft.)

E.C. Flitcroft was the first mechanic to offer free air in Seaside Park. The pump was driven by a one-cylinder Cadillac engine. Prior to the installment of an underground gas pump in 1915, the gasoline was kept in a storage tank inside the garage. (Courtesy Sterling Flitcroft.)

E.C. Flitcroft parked 100 cars a night in his garage at 75¢ each. According to his son Sterling, "Cars were finished with paint and varnished and the finish was not durable. All trim was brass which needed polishing to keep it bright. You could not keep them outside overnight so summer visitors paid us to put them inside." (Courtesy Sterling Flitcroft.)

Tourists would also store their automobiles with the Flitcrofts for the winter. They left their cars at the shore to be used in the summer only. The cars were kept indoors as much as possible to preserve the finish. In 1924 there was such a large demand for space to store cars that private garages were built across Central Avenue from the Modern Garage. The building is still there, and is still used for storage. (Courtesy Sterling Flitcroft.)

The Southern Esso Station, at the northeast corner of Ninth and Central Avenues, was owned by the Flitcroft family beginning in 1931. Peter Cooper rented the business during the summer for many seasons. When the Modern Garage was sold to Venice Amusements c. 1960, Sterling Flitcroft took over the year-round operation of the Southern Esso Station, adding service bays in 1962. Paul Wroblewski started working for Sterling in 1964. He leased the business in 1972 and purchased it in 1974. Both of his sons, Paul Jr. and John, take an active part in the operation of the station. (Courtesy Sterling Flitcroft.)

Local businesses decorated with red, white, and blue banners and bunting for celebrations, including Independence Day, town anniversaries, and the opening of the new Bay Bridge in May 1927. Cowdrick's Garage, located on Fifth Avenue next to Lippincott's store, was one of many service stations in Seaside Park. He later moved his business to the south side of Fifth Avenue. (Courtesy June Roy.)

Businesses on the west side of Fifth Avenue had to contend with flooding when Barnegat Bay would drench the gravel streets, as seen here in the 1920s. Beyond the gas pumps located along the curb is the Bay View Lodge. On the right is the Shibe summer home. Shibe was owner of the Philadelphia Phillies and is the man after whom Shibe Park in Philadelphia is named. (Courtesy Gladys Mathis.)

Thomas H. Devlin's plumbing business was located between Sixth and Seventh Avenues on West Central Avenue opposite the railroad station, c. 1910. Prior to 1920 the building was raised to allow room for both the business and the family home.

The first meat market in Seaside Park was located in the Hiawatha Hotel. The second general store in Sea Side Park was E.W. Shinn and Company, located between Second and Third Avenues in the old Thompson Building. Seen here in 1906 are, from left to right, unidentified, Mr. Welkinson, F. William Greger Sr., Bob Donahue, E. W. Shinn, Ruth Bagley, Howard Jestice, unidentified, and William H. Cowdrick.

Shown here is the interior of E.W. Shinn and Co., c. 1906, with an unidentified man, F. William Greger Sr. (center), and Ruth Bagley (right). Bill Greger Sr. would later open the White Oak Market.

The Shinn family later sold out to Messick and Hayes, southerners who had two helpers. They would play the banjo and guitar while Bill Jones would tap dance and jig. This was the borough's sole winter entertainment for a long time. Early employees included, from left to right, Bob Donahue, E.W. Shinn, Ruth Bagley, William H. Cowdrick, Mr. Welkinson, Howard Jestice, and unidentified.

The Blue Front Market was opened in May 1915 by Andrew J. Doherty in Wickham's building at Third and Central Avenues. He was the first person in Seaside Park to open a fruit store and one of the first to sell packaged liquor. He later moved to Fourth Avenue and opened this larger market. Andrew Doherty is on the far right. (Courtesy Florence Doherty.)

The White Oak Market was opened by F. William Greger Sr. in 1913. His daughter Dorothy was born in the apartment above the store, indicated by the "X" mark. He named his store the "White Oak Market" to give residents a symbolic tree. Seaside Park was originally named "Park City" and had a large park in the center of town. This name was abandoned when the pioneers discovered that mainland trees, including the white oak, would not grow in the sandy soil and harsh environment of the barrier island. (Courtesy Dorothy Greger Mueller.)

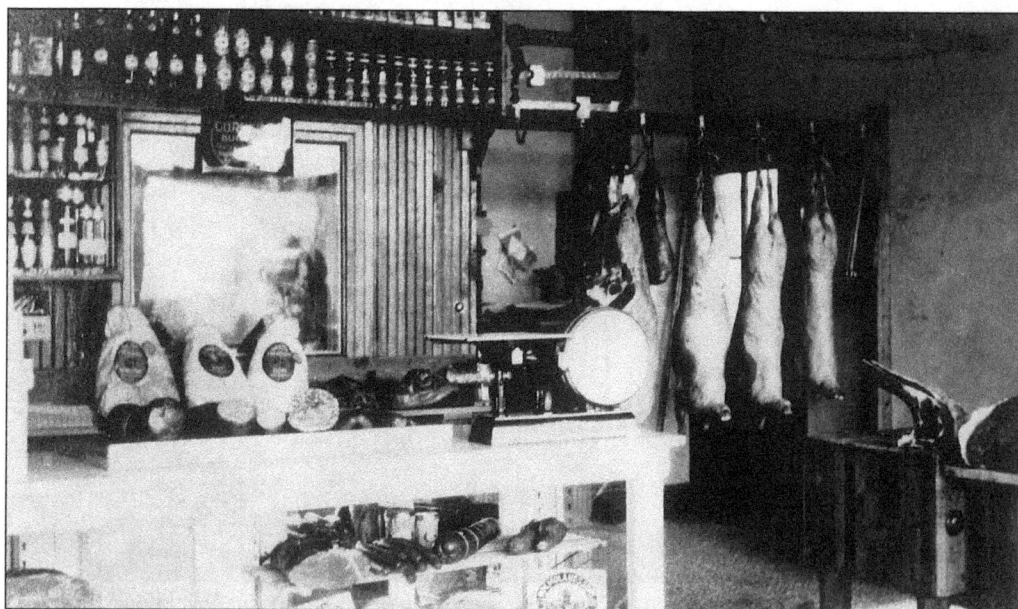

The White Oak Market was one of the most popular meat markets on the barrier island. Milk was sold for 10¢ a quart, and sandwiches were 5¢. The meats were shipped in by train from Philadelphia. (Courtesy Dorothy Greger Mueller.)

From left to right, F. William Greger Sr., William Bates of Cedar Brook, and Alfred Norcross of Chester, Pennsylvania, stand in front of the original White Oak Market after a day of hunting. (Courtesy F. William Greger Jr.)

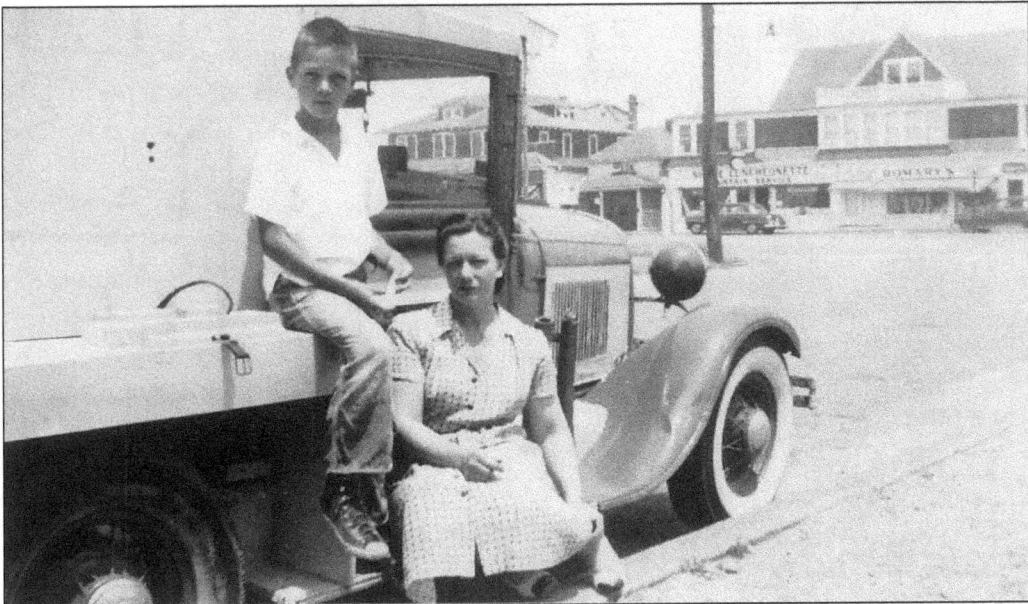

Dorothy Greger Mueller and Guy Mueller are sitting on Uncle Bill's Ford Model A Beach Buggy, which was parked in front of Bill Greger Jr.'s home on the southwest corner of Central and Third Avenues in 1953. In the background is Romary's and the Shore Luncheonette, in the old Thompson building. (Courtesy Guy Mueller.)

In 1927, the White Oak Market moved to its present location between Second and Third Avenues on Central Avenue. F. William Greger's son, Bill Jr., was already a butcher in the family business. By 1932 he was being paid $20 a week. Bill Greger would later run the store until he retired in 1975. (Courtesy F. William Greger Jr.)

In 1933, F. William Greger Sr. applied for and was granted a liquor license. Four years later, the White Oak Liquor Shop was built next to the market. His daughter Dorothy later ran the store. It is currently owned by his grandson, Guy Mueller, making it the oldest family-owned business in Seaside Park. (Courtesy Guy Mueller.)

The White Oak Market delivered their goods up and down the barrier island. Seen here in 1941, the delivery truck is parked on Central Avenue in front of the store. In the background is the fire siren tower, the Bill Greger house, and the red-brick schoolhouse. (Courtesy Julia Greger.)

The White Oak Liquor Shop, aside from advertising the wines and beers, is also displaying a poster for the annual Tournament of Fish fishing contest in this 1961 view. (Courtesy Guy Mueller.)

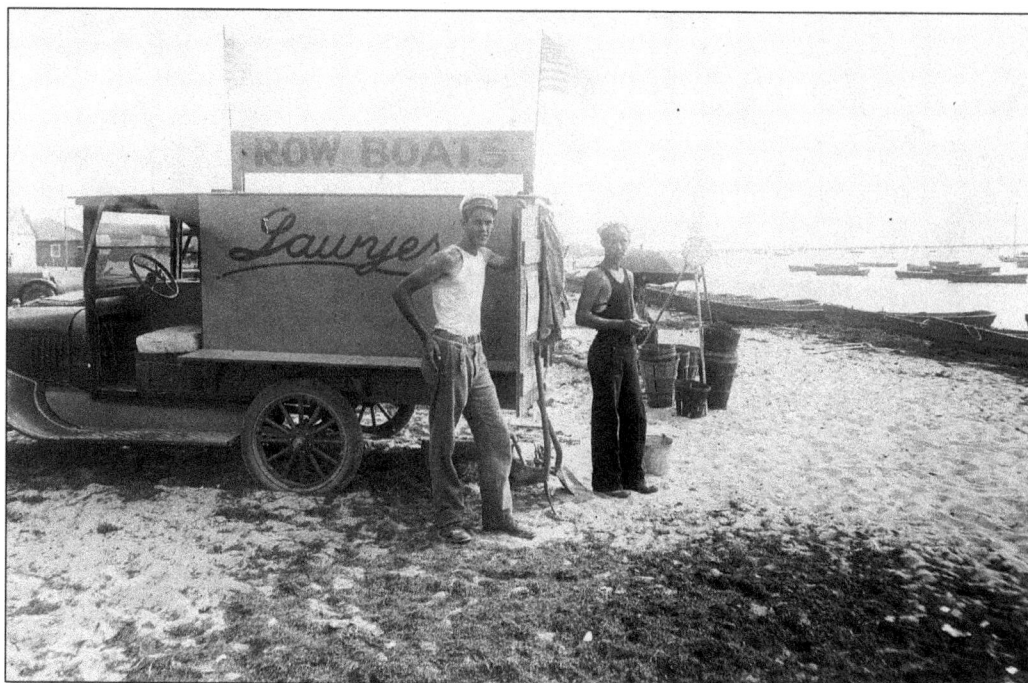

Boat concessions were a successful industry from the 1920s to the early 1970s. Located along the bay shore, they rented boats to tourists for fishing and crabbing. Shown here are Millard Erwin (left) and Edward Kretchman at Howard Lawyer's Row Boats. (Courtesy Millard Erwin.)

Devlin's Boats and Refreshments, located at Thirteenth and Bayview Avenues, was established in 1924 and operated by the family until 1942. (Courtesy F. William Greger Jr.)

Hopper's Basin, located at J Street and the bay in 1900, was later purchased by Yacht Club Commodore William D. Stanger. He renamed it the Seaside Park Boat and Marine Supply Company, where he sold boating supplies, and the Berkeley Yacht Basin for the boat harbor and storage area. His general manager was Captain Eli Townsend, builder of the champion sloop *IHYC*, the sloops *Josephine* and *Empress*, and the cat boat *Virginia*. (Courtesy Dorothy Thomas.)

The Berkeley Yacht Basin was sold to the Thomas family, grandfather Bert D., father Richard O., and son Richard B., in October 1941. At that time there were only 27 boat slips. The Berkeley Yacht Basin became well known and respected for its service, and by the time the basin was sold in 1970, there were 200 boat slips. (Courtesy Dorothy Thomas.)

The Berkeley Yacht Basin was devastated by fire on March 29, 1942. (Courtesy June Roy.)

Although all appeared lost, the Thomas family rebuilt the yard. In the early 1970s, the Berkeley Pool was built between I and J Streets on West Central Avenue. This gigantic swimming pool was open for about a decade. A new boat showroom and warehouse were also constructed. (Courtesy June Roy.)

The Lewis Lumber Company, J Street and Central Avenue, provided lumber and coal during Seaside Park's formative years. The store was purchased and expanded upon by the A.B. Newbury Company about 1930. (Courtesy Ocean County Historical Society.)

With the end of World War II, the A.B. Newbury Company branched out to meet the needs of the building boom. A display room was constructed across from the lumberyard on East Central Avenue between J and K Streets, and offered a variety of appliances needed for the newly built houses. This building was later used as a restaurant and then a design office. It was vacant for many years before being demolished by the First National Bank of Toms River. (Courtesy Richard Steele.)

The Park Market, located on the southwest corner of Porter Avenue and the Boulevard, was opened by Joe Gialanella in 1950. He and his wife, Eleanor, operated the business until about 1976. They sold barbecued chicken, assorted salads, hot fruit pies, Italian sausages, groceries and produce, frozen foods, delicatessen products, household items, and newspapers. Like many "Mom and Pop" stores in Seaside Park, Joe and Eleanor worked 18-hour days in the summer and 12-hour days in the winter. The market, now owned by Joseph and Ruta Didzbalis and Ruta's sister, Vida Melinis, continues to be operated as a family enterprise. (Courtesy Joe Didzbalis.)

Seven

VOLUNTEERS AND PROFESSIONALS

The northwest corner of Fourth and Central Avenues was once the hub of government activity in the borough of Sea Side Park. On the right is the first borough hall. Council meetings had previously been held in the dining room of the mayor's home. The borough hall housed the municipal office, town lock-up, and police station. In 1927, mayor and council leased the school annex, seen here on the far left, as the new borough hall, while the original building was used by the police and courts. The firehouse was built shortly after the founding of the Seaside Park Volunteer Fire Company in 1913. In 1953, a new town hall was built for the municipal offices and police and fire departments at the former site of the railroad station. (Courtesy Gary Madden.)

Early members of the volunteer fire company included, from left to right, Horace Lippincott, William Jones, Albert Reed, Carl Haag Jr., William Greger Sr., John Graham, Tom Devlin, Chief Frank Hewitt, William Bates, Clifford Brown, Aaron Wilbert, and Frank Brockway. The Seaside Park Volunteer Fire Company was founded on May 2, 1913, with Mayor Watson Mathis elected president and Hewitt elected chief.

The first team of horses used by the fire company belonged to Chief Frank Hewitt, who operated the town's express delivery service. The firemen were, from left to right, William Gates, unidentified, Thomas Devlin, Bert Reed, Frank Sprague, William Greger Sr., William Jones, Carl Haag, unidentified, Horace Lippincott Sr., unidentified, Chief Hewitt, Albert Wilbert, and Frank Brockway.

Grand Opening ^ Bridge Seaside Heights to Toms River "Parade" 1912

The fire company participated in the grand opening celebrations of the Bay Bridge, about 1914. In the background is the Hiawatha Hotel and Thompson's Department Store. Others in the parade include Devlin Plumbing and Graham Groceries.

By the time of the second Bay Bridge Dedication Parade in 1927, the fire company had two motorized engines, both REO Speed Wagons. From left to right are Edward Newman, William Bates, unidentified, Frank Hewitt, Roy Koch, Chief William Burdge, and Clifford Brown. (Courtesy William Burdge.)

This is the original firehouse as it looked on January 18, 1954. The addition to the rear of the firehouse was originally used as horse stables. The fire engines had been moved to the new town hall the previous year. The original borough hall was moved on November 20, 1953, from the corner of Fourth and Central Avenues to J Street, where it was rededicated as the "Boy Scout Building." (Courtesy Guy Mueller.)

In 1955, the fire company purchased a 750-gallon Oren pumper. Fire companies from throughout Ocean County joined in the traditional housing celebration for this new apparatus. (Courtesy Millard Erwin.)

The members of the Ladies Auxiliary in January 1968 were, from left to right, as follows: (front row) Peggy Stalb, Frances Hodulich, Mrs. Hodulich, Pat Ridge, Julia Greger, Gertrude Johnson, and Eleanor Ridge: (middle row) Gail Anderson, Betty Jane Matejkowski, Delores Kruttschnitt, Shelby Baran, Margaret Magee, Carol Wroblewski, Ronnie Balfrey, and Molly Devlin; (back row) Gretchen Mitchell, Selena Burdge, Gladys Tracy, Karol Penn, and Barbara Greger.

The fire company SCUBA/Rescue Team posed on March 27, 1977. Former councilman and Assistant Fire Chief Gary Greger, son of Bill and Julia Greger and the husband of Deputy Borough Clerk Barbara Greger, passed away the day after this picture was taken. From left to right they are as follows: (in the boat) Paul Wroblewski Sr., Joel Varga, and Don McLaughlin Sr.; (back row) Mike Bruzzone, Gary Greger Sr., Jack Moyse, Jim Mockaitis, Guy Mueller, Jeff Weist, and Carl Sless. (Courtesy Seaside Park Fire Company.)

The Tri-Boro First Aid Squad was founded in January 1938. During the first year of operation, the squad rendered assistance in 83 emergency calls and 68 silent transportation calls, traveling a total distance of 6,000 miles. The first squad building, shown here on J Street, was completed in 1939. (Courtesy Ocean County Historical Society.)

The first ambulance was a ten-year-old Studebaker purchased from the Point Pleasant First Aid Squad. It was first housed in Flitcroft's garage before the J Street building was constructed, with volunteers answering first aid calls in the three towns originally covered by the squad: Seaside Park, Seaside Heights, and Lavallette. Lavallette soon organized its own first aid squad, and Tri-Boro added the borough of Island Beach to its coverage area. (Courtesy Ocean County Historical Society.)

The first patient of the Tri-Boro First Aid Squad was C. Vernon Sparks, who had suffered a heart attack. The ambulance was in Point Pleasant to be painted, yet responded to the call for assistance at record speeds. The squad assisted Dr. Samuel Tilles in saving Sparks's life. (Courtesy Ocean County Historical Society.)

In 1940, two more ambulances were acquired, a LaSalle and a secondhand Buick. The LaSalle was advertised as "one of the finest in New Jersey, the body custom built, equipped to carry four persons . . . with running water and the cot equipped with an airflow mattress." Another Buick was purchased in 1948 and a Cadillac was bought in 1953.

A drill on March 23, 1960, demonstrated the skills of the first aid squad. From left to right are Aaron "Duffy" Wilbert, Ken Baker (in the plaid hat), Foster Haines, an unidentified victim, and Andy Klee. (Photo by Sam Conover.)

The Tri-Boro First Aid Squad dedicated a 1962 Cadillac in May of that year. The Lavallette First Aid Squad participated in the ceremony. From left to right are Roman A. Birchler, Robert Wenzel, Nathaniel Skinner, John Cagni, Gerald Johnson, Andrew Klee, and President Jesse Anderson. (Photo by Sam Conover, courtesy Jesse Anderson.)

80

Membership in the Tri-Boro First Aid Squad decreased during World War II, when only 7 of the 21 members were on hand to serve the 3 communities. Today, the squad has more than 60 members. (Courtesy Gary Madden.)

Construction on a new squad building began in March 1971 and the building was dedicated on Saturday, December 16, 1972. The squad continues to update their equipment and replace older vehicles. (Courtesy Ocean County Historical Society.)

The first public school was built on Fourth Avenue in 1902. Augustus Voigt taught students from Sea Side Park, Seaside Heights, and Lavallette. Classes went up to the eighth grade. Prior to that, classes were held in a small room over the general store, with Stella Jeffrey as teacher. Other early "schools" included the Fifth Avenue Hotel and the Kennedy House on North Avenue.

The Sea Side Park Public School Class of 1906 consisted of, from left to right, the following: (front row) Helen Brockway, Grace Dunham, Ruth Bagley, teacher Augustus Voigt, Harry Clayton, and Carl Haag; (back row) Ray Clayton, Estella Hewitt, Helen Dunham, Harriet Longstreet, Ella Clayton, Sadie Wilbur, and Bill Cowdrick. (Courtesy Alice Burdge.)

The 1916 graduating class from the Seaside Park Public School consisted of, from left to right, Joel Brower, Amanda Brown, Mary Clayton, Margaret Van Note, Julia Thompson, and Charles Miller. This was one of the first classes to attend the Toms River High School the following year. (Courtesy Kathryn Sprague.)

Beatrice Driscoll, who later married Joseph Penrose, stands on the steps of the Seaside Park Public School in 1922. The school addition seen here was completed in 1917, and would later serve as town hall. After 1953, the building was returned to school use as a classroom annex. (Courtesy Beatrice Penrose.)

The red-brick schoolhouse was built to the west of the old school in 1927. The basement floor often flooded during high tide in Barnegat Bay. The schoolhouse was used up until 1970, when the new school opened on the northwest corner of Fourth and Central Avenues. (Courtesy Ocean County Historical Society.)

The Seaside Park Safety Patrol, shown here on the front steps of the red-brick schoolhouse in December 1939, consisted of the following, from left to right: (front row) Robert Johnson, John Larsen, Russell Norcross, Harry Van Sciver, and Samuel Hodulich; (back row) Mabel Thornes, Elsie Jackson, Patsy Aiken, and Jean Reilly.

Lester Gerhard, seen here in 1937, was hired as the principal and teacher of grammar grades at the Seaside Park Public School in 1928. He maintained his position as principal and teacher until his death in May 1957. (Courtesy Tess Schwimmbeck.)

The school staff in June 1952 was comprised of the following, from left to right: (front row) Ann McGee, Bertha Swaim, and Maryann Yetman: (back row) John Novello, Wilmer "Tiny" Johnson Sr., Grace Dare, Lester Gerhard, and George Dare. "Tiny" Johnson, the powerful janitor with a heart of gold, would entertain the schoolchildren by lifting them in garbage cans with one hand and spinning them as on a make-shift carousel. (Courtesy Gail Anderson.)

The first church in Sea Side Park was the Union Church, nicknamed the "Chapel By the Sea." Built in 1899 on the southeast corner of Fourth and Central Avenues, the Union Church was nondenominational, for all to worship at. Prior to construction of the chapel, services were held in the Manhasset Hotel. Sunday school classes were held in the Bouwd House with chairs borrowed from the Hiawatha Hotel.

Chapel, Seaside Park, N. J.

The first minister at the Union Church was Rev. Blake, seen here by the front door of the recently completed chapel. He conducted Protestant services at eleven o'clock in the morning. Catholic Masses were held at eight o'clock on Sunday mornings during the summer months from 1905 to 1911. African-American residents worshiped Sunday evenings. (Courtesy Julia Brower.)

The Union Church, at left, was located close to the Yacht Club, railroad station, and Hiawatha Hotel (at right). The Bouwd House, the first building built in Seaside Park in 1867, can be seen in the background, to the left of the hotel. It was built by Isaac Jennings of Cedar Run and later sold to George and Charles Bouwd of Philadelphia.

The Union Church was once the hub of social life for young people. Vacation Bible School, held for two weeks during the summer, attracted dozens of children. This photograph was taken about 1946. (Courtesy Gretchen Mitchell.)

The St. Catharine of Siena Church had its beginnings in 1905, when Rev. Gregory Scheuermann, a member of the Franciscan Order of Friars Minor Convectual, was vacationing in Sea Side Park. He held an informal Catholic Mass in a Fourth Avenue cottage, with a Mass the following Sunday in the Union Church. Francis P. Larkin Sr. donated land for a church to be built upon in 1908. It was completed in 1912. (Courtesy Bill Greger.)

On December 22, 1922, Franciscan Fathers moved into St. Catharine's Rectory, constructed on the north side of E Street, behind the church. Eight years later, a parish hall was built to the east of the rectory and used for social purposes and as an auditorium for Sunday Masses during July and August. (Courtesy Kate Smith.)

Groundbreaking for the construction of the new St. Catharine of Siena Church occurred on the Feast of Saint Francis, October 4, 1953. Father Gebhard Braungart is holding the shovel while church and civic dignitaries look on. The new church seats 1,200 people. It was dedicated April 17, 1955. The old church was dismantled, with the windows being sent to Costa Rica and the interior shipped to Albany, New York.

May Day celebrations, such as this one in the late 1940s, were always popular. From left to right are Mary Miller, Doris Batten, Barbara Derocco, Lorraine Colvin, and Theresa Schwimmbeck. (Courtesy Tess Schwimmbeck.)

From the time of Sea Side Park's incorporation in 1898, marshals were employed to maintain law and order during the summer months in the area. They would police the town, originally on foot, and later on motorcycles or in cars. Appointments were made by council on a yearly basis. One of the first marshals was Frank Sprague, who was first hired in 1912 and held the position until 1931. (Courtesy Seaside Park Police Department).

Clifford R. Brown, known simply as "the Chief," was in charge of the police department from 1931 through 1967. He was also the fire chief for many years, often finding himself wearing both hats at a fire. As was written in the *Sunshine News* in 1948, in reference to an increase of civilians following fire engines to a call, "Chief of Fire Department Clifford R. Brown says if it continues, Chief of Police Clifford R. Brown will be forced to issue summons." (Courtesy Seaside Park Police Department.)

Shown here are the 1938 Lifeguard Champions from Seaside Park. These underdogs faced incredible odds against beach patrols from Cape May, Atlantic City, Wildwood, Ocean City, and Jones Beach, yet were declared the champions of the entire East Coast. They are, from left to right, as follows: (front row) William A. Hiering, Albert Hiering, Raymond Stone, and Charles Miller; (back row) John Peterson Sr., Chester Johnson, Captain William T. Hiering, Gordon Eisemann and Albert Wilbert. Not in the photograph is L. Burke Cousart. (Courtesy John Peterson.)

The 1957 Seaside Park beach patrol lifeguards shown here are, from left to right: (front row) J. Stumpf, Jack Perrine, Ron Locandro, unidentified, Bill Gatti, Kent Laufer, Frank Pizzi, John Applegate, Joe Gatti, and Captain Jerry Bannigan; (back row) Charles Righter, Larry Larkin, Art Thompson, Rich Toaldo, Ray Stumpf, Hank Owens, Bob Kennedy, Roger Locandro, Tom Urbanik, Frank Wagner, and Pete Moracco. (Photograph by Sam Conover, courtesy Joanna Pearson.)

Eight

GROWING UP IN SEASIDE PARK

One of the oldest pictures of Sea Side Park was taken approximately 1897, looking west from the oceanfront. The two houses in the foreground are 48 I Street and 34 I Street. The streets were sand and only marked with the narrow boardwalks along each road. The pump house seen at the rear of the center home was located behind the southeast corner of the present Tri-Boro First Aid Squad Building. The Berkeley Railroad Station, built to accommodate those staying at the Berkeley Arms Hotel, is the building at the right. (Courtesy William Schoettle.)

Tent City was a unique camp below the water tower on Thirteenth Avenue. In the early 1920s, Frank Fearnley built a small cooking shack and, with the permission of Mayor Horace Lippincott, staked out tents. The campers utilized the sanitary facilities in the firehouse ten blocks north of the camp before the borough installed facilities for the campers. Many of the early Tent City residents liked the area so much they decided to buy property in Seaside Park and built cottages. (Courtesy Bill Greger.)

The first pioneers to Seaside Park brought livestock with them. Residents had cows, horses, and chickens for milk, transportation, and food. The area south of Ninth Avenue was nicknamed "Roosterville" because of all the poultry. Loud choruses from dozens of roosters woke residents at sunrise. (Courtesy Julia Brower.)

94

Horse-drawn wagons were used for transportation before automobiles came to town in 1911. Bakery goods from Philadelphia were unloaded at the Sea Side Park Station and carted to the various markets throughout town. The horses were also used during emergencies to pull the fire equipment. (Courtesy Charlie Martowlis.)

Many of the borough services, including water, sewerage, and garbage, went to the lowest bidder with very unsatisfactory, and at times, disastrous results. In 1916, borough employees became responsible for the building of and repairs to the boardwalk; carting back to the beach sand which had blown onto Ocean Avenue, at that time a gravel road; the collection of garbage; and the development and care of water pipes and the sewerage system. Above is the public works's General Motors truck. (Courtesy Charlie Martowlis.)

The children of Seaside Park enjoyed playing in the fire gong. From left to right are Florence Thompson, Mildred Bagley, Katie Brower, and Julia Thompson, about 1912. In the background is the schoolyard, looking north. (Courtesy Ellen Marzulli.)

The "neighborhood gang" in 1924 were, from left to right, Florence Carlson, Margaret Endresen, Mary Devlin, Geneva Endresen, Ann Endresen, and Joe Devlin. (Courtesy Joe Devlin.)

The *Ariella* and the *Dorianna* were sister boats used to transport residents and visitors from Seaside Park to Island Heights, on the mainland. They were also used for weekend excursions and sightseeing tours of Barnegat Bay. (Courtesy Charlie Martowlis.)

Moonlight cruises from Toms River to Seaside Park were common in the early 1900s. The Seaside Park Volunteer Fire Company often sold tickets for cruises on the *Ariella* and *Dorianna* to raise funds for their organization. (Courtesy Charlie Martowlis.)

This house at 131 I Street was once the home of the Hughes family. Fire Chief Ron Redy and his wife, Barbara, and their son Josh live there now. (Courtesy Bill Greger.)

These ladies have joined together on the porch of 58 N Street to relax in the afternoon breeze as they hold their quilting bee. (Courtesy Dorothy Thomas.)

Seaside Park pioneer E.C. Flitcroft, shown here standing on the bumper of his Modern Garage truck, is all smiles during the 50th anniversary parade for Seaside Park in 1948. (Courtesy Ocean County Historical Society.)

Sterling Flitcroft, son of E.C. Flitcroft, is shown here before the storm of November 16, 1935. The wide tires on his beach buggy helped give traction on the soft sand. (Courtesy Ocean County Historical Society.)

In the early 1900s, dozens of workers hauled sand from the oceanfront to fill in the low-lying marshes of Fifth Avenue to make buildable property. (Courtesy June Roy.)

The Greger house, home of F. William "Uncle Bill" Greger and his wife, Julia, is shown here in 1930. Located on the southwest corner of Third and Central Avenues, it was purchased by the board of education in 1988 and converted into office and storage space for the neighboring elementary school. (Courtesy Guy Mueller.)

National Guardsmen were sent to guard the Pennsylvania Railroad Bridge during World War I. This photograph was taken in front of Frank Hewitt's real estate office, which was later used as an ice house. From left to right are Bill Gray, Tommy Meehan, Albert Trotter, Tommy Mendal, and an unidentified soldier.

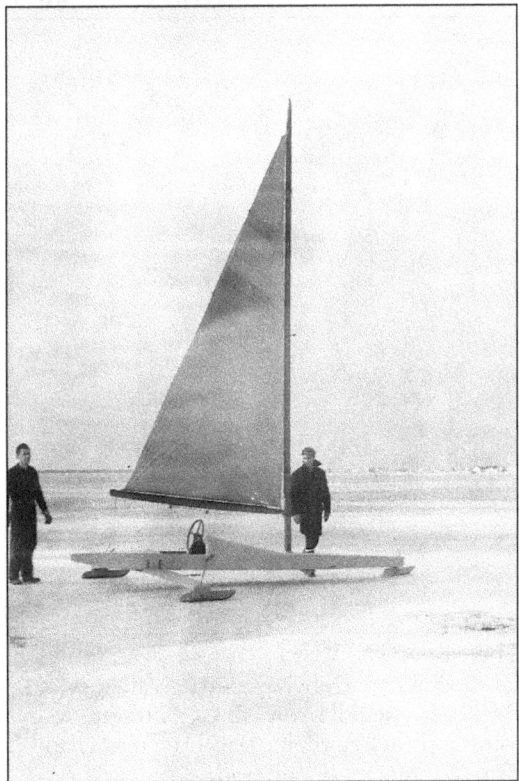

Barnegat Bay often froze solid in the early 1900s. In addition to supplying ice for the fisheries, the bay provided recreation for the townsfolk. Seen here is an ice boat.

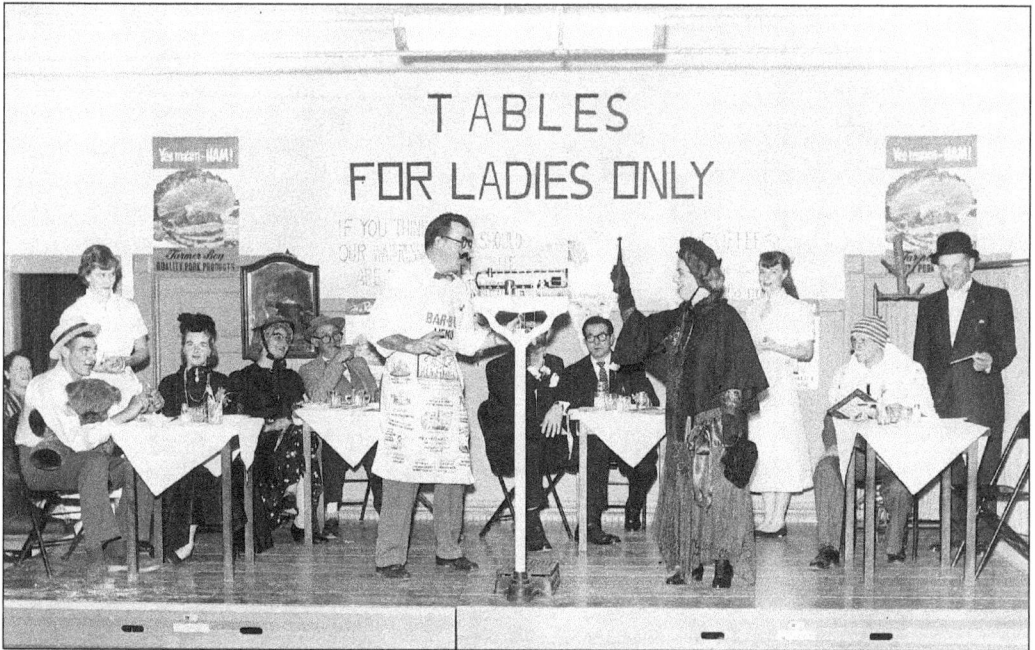

Scenes in a Restaurant was one of the one-act plays presented by the Little Theater Group. Pictured are, from left to right, Glenn Erwin, Betty Jane Matejkowski, Vi Hoffman, Laura Erwin, Al Erwin, Don Whiteman, Joe Pinelli, Otto Fishbein, Vi Verdier, Hazel Bearmore, Oliver Tatum, and Anthony Villani. (Courtesy Vi Verdier.)

The cast of *This Way to Heaven* were, from left to right: (front row) Agnes Polhemus, Eleanor Graff, Madora Doherty, Betty Waller, Vi Hoffman, Molly Miller, Linda Mescoe, and Rita Boekholt; (middle row) E.C. Flitcroft, Maryann Yetman, Helen Cobb, Elaine Swayze, Vi Verdier, Ethel Fairfield, Bob Davenport, and Leo Kiernan; (back row) Malcolm Fairfield and Don Whiteman. (Courtesy Vi Verdier.)

The *Graf Zeppelin* flies over J Street in 1928. The Navy base at Lakehurst, home of Hanger One and site of the *Hindenburg* disaster, housed dirigibles and blimps. Lighter than air ships frequently traveled over Seaside Park on their way to the airstrips at Lakehurst. (Courtesy Sterling Flitcroft.)

The Tenth Avenue beach was proudly represented during the 50th anniversary parade in 1948. In the background are the Mayfair Apartments, Ocean Avenue, and O Street. The apartments were destroyed in the great March storm of 1962. (Courtesy Ocean County Historical Society.)

The Coast Guard tower, located on the oceanfront opposite the Coast Guard Station on Decatur Avenue, was used into the 1960s. After the tower was demolished, the footings for the tower were used as the foundation for the Seaside Park Beach Patrol Headquarters. (Courtesy Ocean County Historical Society.)

The boardwalk and amusements of Seaside Park and Seaside Heights have been an attraction to families for several generations. The carousel seen here was destroyed by fire in 1955. The blaze was reported by the guardsman in the lookout tower on Decatur Avenue. (Courtesy June Roy.)

This is an aerial view of Seaside Park in 1940, looking north. In the upper right is the train station. Ninth Avenue is the first horizontal street, showing the homes of Judge Russell Conover (center of photograph) and Millard and Edith Erwin (on the south side of Ninth Avenue, with the fenced-in backyard). The house on the lower right was built by Millard Erwin in 1936 and insulated with Sword eel grass. (Courtesy Harlon Conover.)

The South Seaside Park/Seaside Park border is seen here about 1955. Although the tracks were removed in 1949, the outline of where the railroad once curved north is still visible. The department of public works building can be seen under the water tower at Thirteenth Avenue. (Courtesy William Coles.)

This view was taken looking north during the late 1950s. In the foreground is the Hiawatha Hotel and Modern Garage. The field in the lower left is now the school playground. (Courtesy Charlie Martowlis.)

This is the northern end of Seaside Park, during the late 1950s. Berkeley Harbor is in the upper left portion of the photograph. The Mathis Baths and apartments are located between Ocean Avenue and the Atlantic. (Courtesy Charlie Martowlis.)

Nine

BEACH AND BOARDWALK

One of Seaside Park's greatest attractions is its almost 2 miles of shoreline. Sunbathers, swimmers, surfers, and fishermen all enjoy the vast stretches of white sandy beach. Time seems to stand still on the beach and boardwalk. This picture, taken by famed photographer Harlon Conover in 1955, could have easily been taken today. (Courtesy Harlon Conover.)

This view of the ocean and beach, taken about 1918, shows the dunes, carousel, and breakers, but no boardwalk. The youngster in the foreground is not identified. (Courtesy Judge Dorothea E. Donaldson.)

The first boardwalk along the oceanfront, built in the early 1900s, was only 4 feet wide. The boardwalk was destroyed by a torrential nor'easter in 1914. It was later rebuilt on pilings so the ocean waves would pass underneath the walk. (Courtesy Dorothy Thomas.)

A stroll on the boardwalk in the early 1900s was certainly more formal than it is today. Ladies always had their parasols, while men wore hats. (Courtesy Dorothy Thomas.)

Elizabeth Marren Perinchief sits with her cat, Muffy, on the ocean beach, c. 1920s. Notice the height of the boardwalk in the background, as it was rebuilt after 1914. Children were once able to walk underneath the decking. Today, the beach has been built up with a line of protective sand dunes. (Courtesy Betty Perinchief.)

The Casino is shown here, from a postcard dated July 31, 1911. Located between North and Island Avenues and the boardwalk, the Casino featured bowling alleys, a dance hall, a lunch counter, a bath house, and a novelty store in the early 1900s. (Courtesy Mike Mangum.)

The Casino was a popular place for families to visit for entertainment. Seen here, Anna Brower enjoys a stroll with her baby carriage on the famous boardwalk of Seaside Park. (Courtesy Anna L. Brower.)

For a short period of time there was a narrow boardwalk along the bayshore from Fifth to Fourteenth Avenue. It was seldom used because of the mosquitoes. Malaria, carried by the insects, was a major concern to the founders of Seaside Park. In the background is the train bridge. (Courtesy Fred Wacker.)

The first merry-go-round in the area, located just over the border of neighboring Seaside Heights and seen here under construction, burned down in 1955. The fire, which started in the carousel building, destroyed three blocks of amusements. (Courtesy Eleanor Peck.)

Sand sculpturing was once a major pastime on the beach. "King Neptune" and "Lending a Hand" were sculpted as part of a contest in Seaside Heights. Meredith Havens, a reporter for the *Trenton Times* newspaper who lived in Seaside Park, was considered a master builder of sand castles.

Fun for children of all ages, a small railroad circled the small stretch of beach between the street and the boardwalk in August 1950. In the background is Phoebe Hiering's apartments. On the left is Coast Guard Station 109, still in service at the time. The apartments were destroyed in the March 1962 storm. (Courtesy Gladys Mathis.)

Mathis Baths, N Street and east of Ocean Avenue, was a private beach with its own bathhouse and concessions. (Courtesy Gladys Mathis.)

The Mathis Bathhouse was destroyed in the infamous March 1962 storm that devastated the entire barrier island. (Courtesy Gladys Mathis.)

On June 9, 1955, a small fire quickly became a major conflagration as a three-block area of beachfront concessions, from Dupont Avenue in Seaside Heights to below Farragut Avenue in Seaside Park, was reduced to ashes. Discovered by the Coast Guard tower watch at 6 a.m., it took several hours of firefighting by most of Ocean County's fire companies and several from Monmouth County to bring the blaze under control. (Courtesy Harlon Conover.)

Beginning the next morning and working nearly round-the-clock at clearing debris and on reconstruction, the concessions were reopened in their concrete buildings for the Fourth of July weekend. (Courtesy Harlon Conover.)

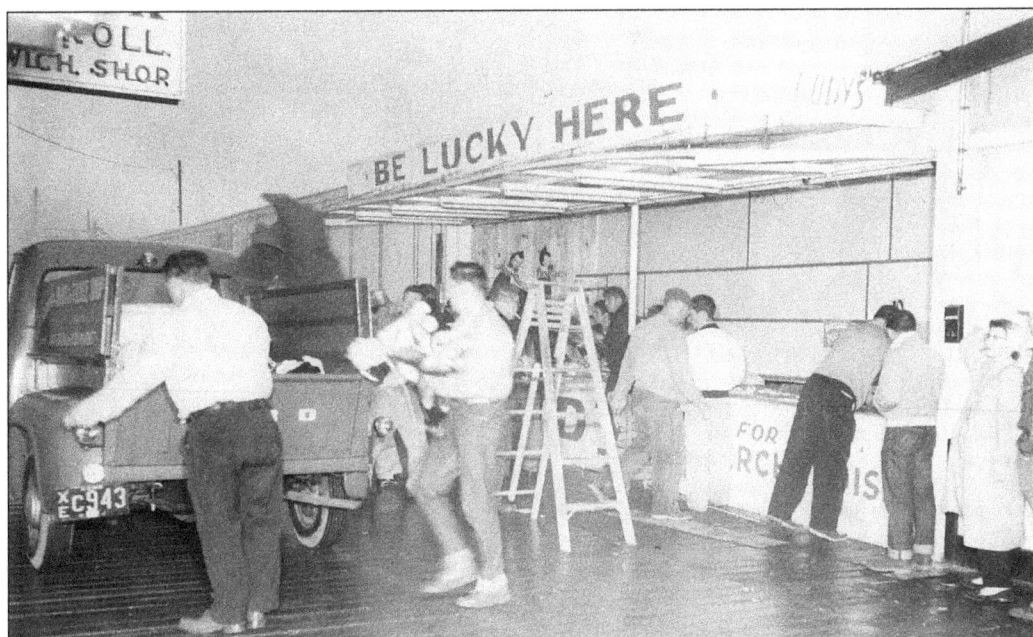

Frank Golumbeski, owner of Frank's Bait and Tackle store, allowed his truck to be used to salvage as much merchandise as possible from the concessions before the fire reached this area. (Courtesy Harlon Conover.)

A dinner was held in the parish hall of St. Catharine's Church to show appreciation to all the firefighters from the two counties who assisted in extinguishing the boardwalk fire. Those serving on the dinner committee were, from left to right, as follows: (front row) Andrew Gabriel, Sanford Lawyer, J. Stanley Tunney, Aaron "Duffy" Wilbert, and Clarence Balfrey; (back row) Henry "Whitey" Lee, Lester Gerhard, Irvin Lees, Millard Erwin, Charles Kessler, and Horace Ridge. (Courtesy Millard Erwin.)

115

Funtown Pier, seen here in 1973, is located on the northern section of the boardwalk. A family amusement center with rides and an arcade, Funtown Pier has a Ferris wheel and, up until the summer of 1997, a log flume. The log flume was dismantled in the spring of 1998 and transported to another amusement area out of the state. (Courtesy Jesse Anderson.)

Ocean and Porter Avenues looking south, seen here in 1973, is the southern section of the boardwalk amusements. On the right is the old Strand Theater, which has since been demolished and turned into a parking lot. (Courtesy Jesse Anderson.)

Ten

Island Beach and the Fish Pounds

Pound fishing was a major industry along the shore from the late 1800s through the early 1950s. The Seaside Park Fish Company at Twenty-Fourth Avenue in the South Seaside Park section of Berkeley Township opened in 1910. Large nets strung between hickory poles in the Atlantic Ocean captured fish which were kept fresh by storing them in cold storage plants on the beach. The fish were then transported to the Fulton Fish Market in New York City and the Dock Street Market in Philadelphia by the Pennsylvania Railroad. The land eventually became more valuable for development and the pound fisheries were replaced by summer homes and condominiums. (Courtesy Gary Madden.)

CHADWICK FISHERY   Bill GREGER

The Chadwick Fishery is shown here in a drawing by the late F. William "Uncle Bill" Greger. The local historian of Seaside Park and a descendent of the Chadwick family, Uncle Bill had a talent for art. Many of his drawings were made on butcher paper at the White Oak Market, where he was a butcher. Uncle Bill never studied art in high school, to the surprise of many residents. A gifted man with a golden heart, Bill Greger passed away in 1987. The Chadwick Fishery was located in the Silver Beach section of Dover Township, north of Seaside Park. (Courtesy the Greger and Mueller families.)

The United Fisheries had a packing shed, ice house, horse stable, and 14-man bunk house. The workers were from the island of Olib, off Yugoslavia. The fishery closed in the fall of 1953. (Courtesy the Greger and Mueller families.)

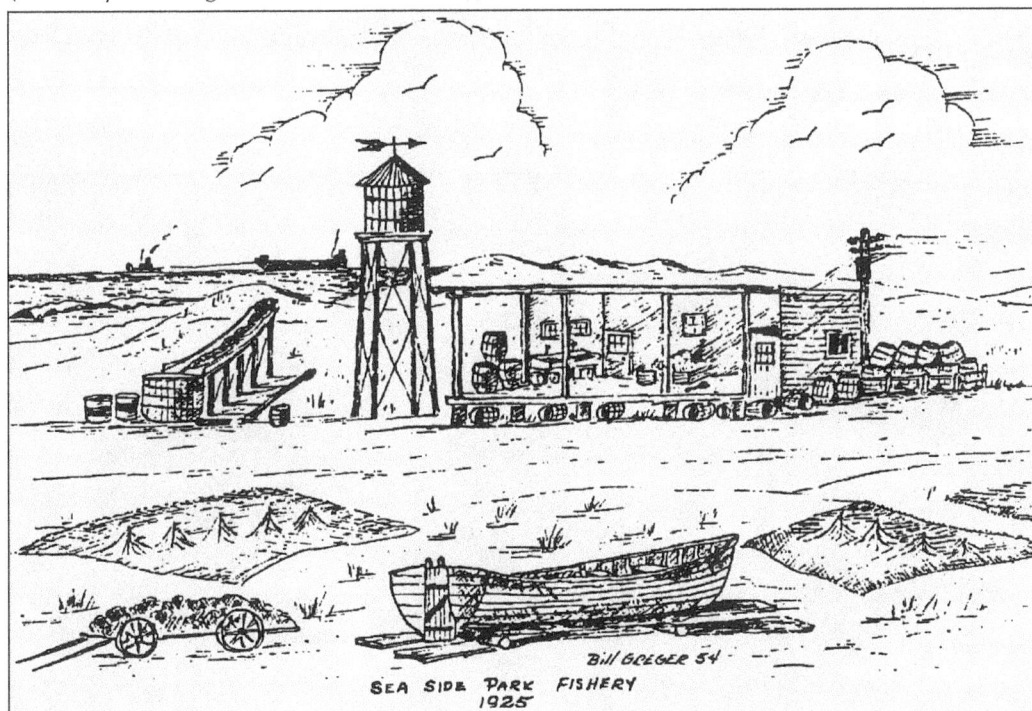

The Sea Side Park Fishery, depicted here in 1925, opened their season in mid-April. In the cold winter months, workers filled the ice house with ice cut from Barnegat Bay. During World War I, the fisheries supplied fish to army cantonments in various parts of the country. (Courtesy the Greger and Mueller families.)

Some of the fishery men posed by their boats on the southern beach of Seaside Park. Fish nets were also located in the ocean off Eleventh through Thirteenth Avenues. (Courtesy Betty Perinchief.)

This bunker boat was photographed off Seaside Park in the 1930s. Moss bunker, or menhaden, was a protein-rich fish used for fertilizer and bait. A large processing plant was located on Crab Island, in Great Bay off Tuckertown. (Courtesy Ocean County Historical Society.)

The United Fisheries on Twenty-Second Avenue in South Seaside Park, shown here in 1941, had three horses and several pound boats, including the *Anna*, *Diana*, and *Helen*. Their nets were located 1.5 nautical miles below the Toms River Coast Guard Station (off of Fourteenth Avenue). (Courtesy Bill Greger.)

Fish caught at the pounds included albacore, blue fish, cod, flounder, herring, mackerel, weakfish, bunker, bass, and eels. Half a load of fish would fill 45 barrels. (Courtesy Bill Greger.)

The pound nets, shown here being inspected for tears, were 75 feet across and 45 feet in height. They were painted with a mixture of kerosene and Baltimore copper paint to help prevent rot, and were changed every 5 to 6 weeks. (Courtesy Francis P. "Sonny" and Dorothy Larkin III.)

Beach buggies and treaded tractors later replaced the teams of horses once used to transport pound boats and baskets of fish. (Courtesy Bill Greger.)

Malinda "Ma" Penn served the pound fisheries and their men for many years with her luncheonette and gasoline station, located at Twentieth and Central Avenues in South Seaside Park. She sold boots, gloves, and other necessities. (Courtesy Fred Penn.)

Ma Penn made clam chowder from fresh bay clams. A big-hearted woman, she gave Christmas gifts to the children of the fishermen. Even the horses knew of her generosity, often trotting to her kitchen door looking for a handout. (Courtesy Fred Penn.)

Eel grass, also known as seaweed, was harvested from Barnegat Bay in the early 1900s. One of the larger operations was run by William Schuster "Bud" Sword at the north end of Island Beach. The Sword family employed approximately ten men to help with the various operations. Long forked rakes were used to pitch the grass up on the beach or onto large flat boats called scows.

Horse-drawn carts carried the grass to the drying racks. Eel grass has a strong hydrogen sulfate odor that disappears when dried, and is practically fireproof. This made seaweed an ideal insulator for buildings and ice boxes; it was also used as packing material for fragile pottery during the early years of this century, and was mixed with horse hair for furniture and mattress stuffing. The upholstery on the first Model-T Fords was even stuffed with eel grass.

The drying racks were made of rot-resistant cedar poles covered with chicken wire. After the grass was completely dried, it was baled in 200-pound bundles and put on a skiff at the Old Inlet Cove, from which it was transported to the Pennsylvania Railroad siding at Twenty-Fourth Street in the South Seaside Park section of Berkeley Township. From there the seaweed went to Philadelphia and New York.

James Brade Sword purchased the original Life Saving Station No. 14 for $50 in 1899 and moved it from the ocean to the bay side of the island. First used as an art studio by James, his son William utilized the cottage as headquarters for his eel grass industry. The industry died out by the 1930s after a blight killed off the grass.

The Reed Hotel, built in 1876 of lumber from wrecked schooners, was located at the northern end of Island Beach. The hotel catered to sportsmen and hunting parties. It was demolished in the early 1900s. (Courtesy Bill Greger.)

The Haring Hotel, also located in the northern section of Island Beach, was built in the early 1800s. Rooms rented for $1 a night. Hunters and fishermen both frequented the hotel, famous for its hospitality and pristine location. The hotel also had a barn, chicken coop, ice house, and garden. (Courtesy Bill Greger.)

The Reed Hotel Ice House, insulated with thick walls of eel grass, stored blocked ice cut from a freshwater spring located north of the hotel. The ice was cut during winter freezes. Ice houses like this one were common along the beach prior to 1913, when the Barnegat Power and Cold Storage Plant was built in Seaside Heights. (Courtesy Bill Greger.)

Bud Sword is seen here, as a young man, sitting on a wrecked ship at Island Beach. Bud's house on Twenty-Third Avenue in South Seaside Park was destroyed by fire several years ago. The windows and contents all burned, yet the walls stood. Between the framing studs was the original, noncombustible eel grass insulation. (Courtesy Bill Greger.)

Elwood "Cap" Colvin and Nick Barulic are shown at the original gatehouse to Island Beach. The State of New Jersey purchased the 2,694-acre property from the heirs of the Phipps Estate in 1953 for $42,750,000. Island Beach State Park opened to the public in 1959. The state park now has over a million visitors a year. It is famous for its bathing beaches, surf fishing, vegetation, and wildlife. (Courtesy Tess Schwimmbeck.)